Stop Tweeting and go to Sleep, Mr. President

Written and illustrated by
John Spreincer McKellyanne Huckamucci

Dedicated to everyone with a crummy boss who makes you look bad no matter what you do and stains your professional reputation for life even though it's not my fault this happened and this probably was my only chance to work at the White House so what was I supposed to do, say no? YOU SAY NO you brave keyboard warrior with 40 Twitter followers, most of them bots who will never respect you because you spend half your workday resenting your jerk co-worker who makes more than you despite spending all day playing Fortnite, sound on with no headphones, in the cube next to you and no one ever says anything about how unfair that is, least of all you. At least I get to be on TV

The fox nestles close to his friends—
Wait, hold on, this episode's a repeat.
You watched it already this afternoon.
Mr. President, it's time to go to sleep.

The windows are dark in D.C.
Your staff huddles down to silently weep.
I'll read you one last story from Infowars
If you promise you'll then go to sleep.

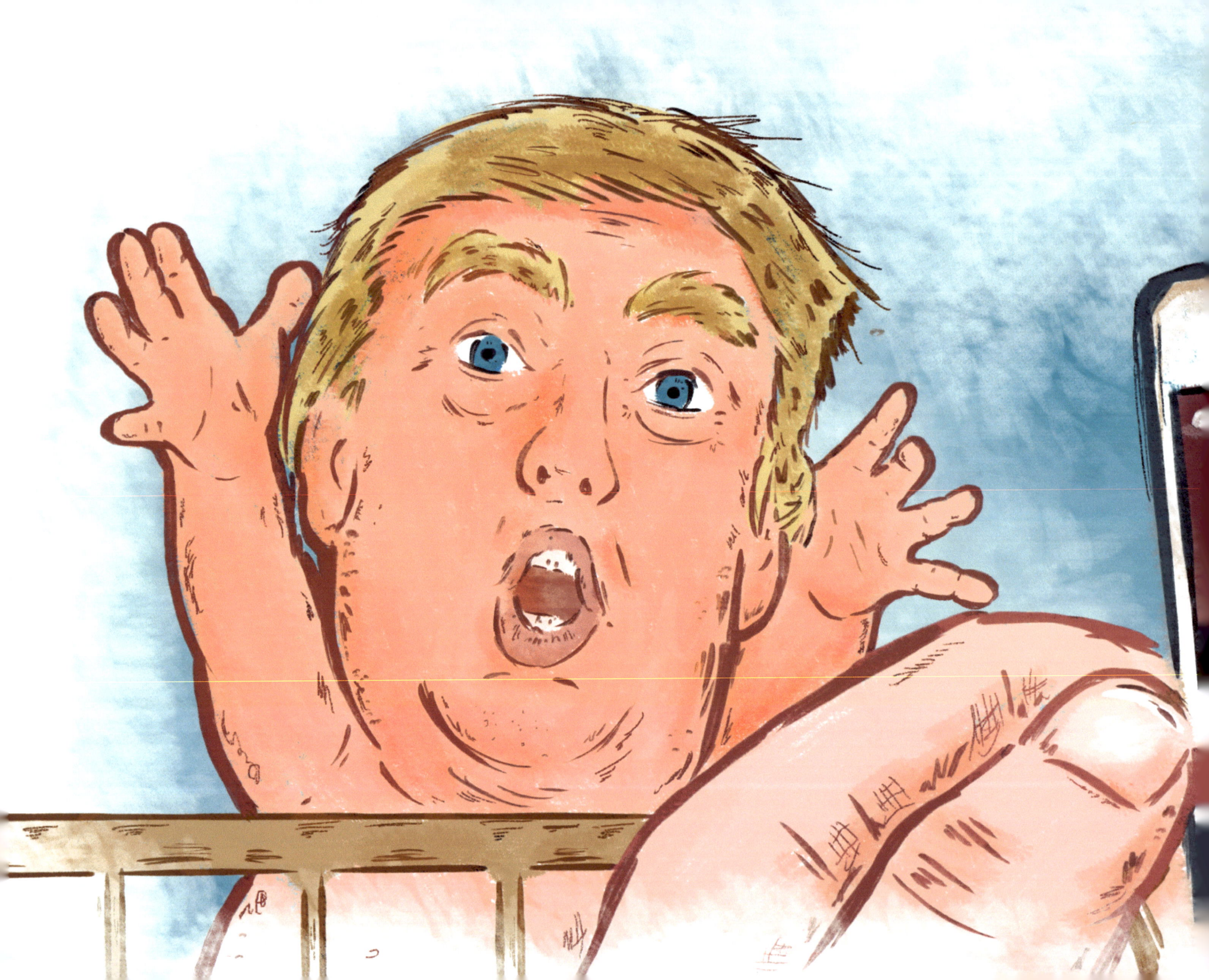

The eagles who **BEEP BEEP**
Ah, geez, a text from Steve.
Your phone didn't unmute itself, sir.
That's ridiculous, stop lying.
Put it down, and please go to sleep.

The wind whis—where in the world are you going.
Lay down. You've got a schedule to keep.
I don't care what ESPN said about you.
Your phone's out of battery and, like you, it really needs some sleep.

The froggie has made—WHAT ARE YOU TYPING
"I'm, like, a really smart person" REALLY??
YOU'RE THE PRESIDENT, not a 12-year-old boy!
And covfefe isn't a word. You're tired and typing nonsense.
Plug the phone in, lay down and get some sleep.

The owls fly fo—oh goodness you can't say that, that is so racist—
WHAT DO YOU MEAN "HOW IS THAT RACIST"
READ WHAT YOU JUST TYPED
OOPS I tripped over your charging cable and tore it, my bad.
Guess you can't send that tweet til morning.
May as well just go to sleep.

The cubs and lions—
WHO in the WORLD
GAVE YOU A BATTERY PACK CASE
Was it Stephen, that Pee Wee Herman-looking creep
What do you mean you "just found it" I'M NOT STUPID!!
Put it away and get some sleep!!

The giant pang—OH MY GOSH dude
Again with this 306 nonsense
Week after week after week after freaking week
YOU WON THE ELECTION*,
WE KNOW, IT'S BEEN ALMOST TWO YEARS
And it feels like twice as long
Since I asked you to GO TO SLEEP.

The seeds slumber beneath—
Wait, what "tapes"
Are there TAPES??
IS COMEY GONNA—
THEN
WHY
IN
THE
WORLD
DID
YOU
TWEET
THAT????

The flowers doze oh geez oh geez oh geez OH GEEZ COME ON
DID YOU JUST DECLARE NUCLEAR WAR IN A TWEET???
HOW IN THE WORLD ARE YOU NOT BANNED FOR THAT
COME ON @JACK
I need to go fix this right now so PLEASE GO THE—
Ah geez he already respo—
LOOK I DON'T KNOW WHAT A DOTARD IS.
HOW ARE YOU CRAZIER THAN HE IS.
GO TO SLEEP.

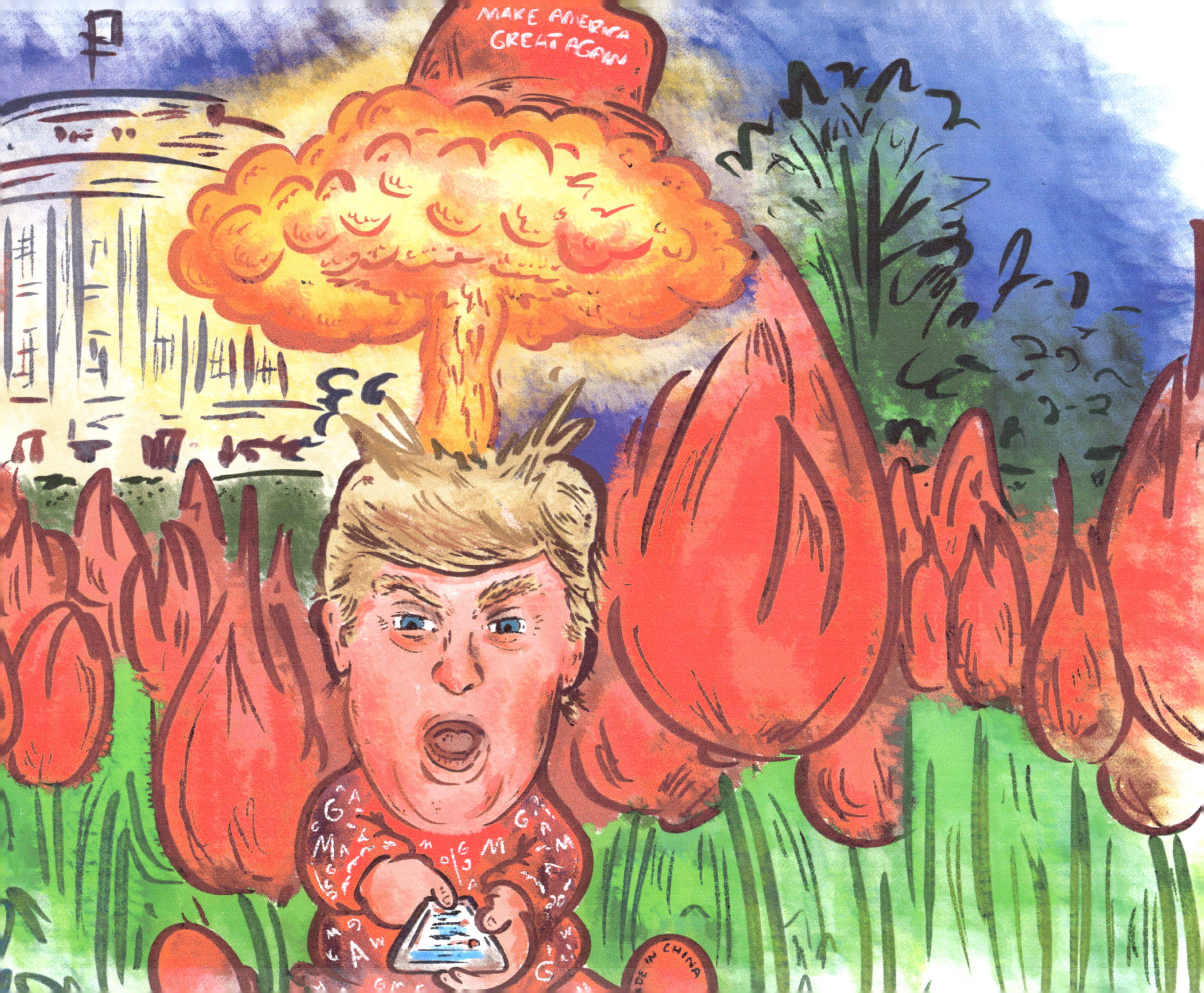
MAKE AMERICA
GREAT AGAIN
ADE IN CHINA

You know what, forget this.
Forget all this. And forget you.
Note to self: Discuss 25th Amendment with Veep.
What's that, sir? Oh, I didn't say anything.
You're overtired and hearing things.
Just close your eyes…

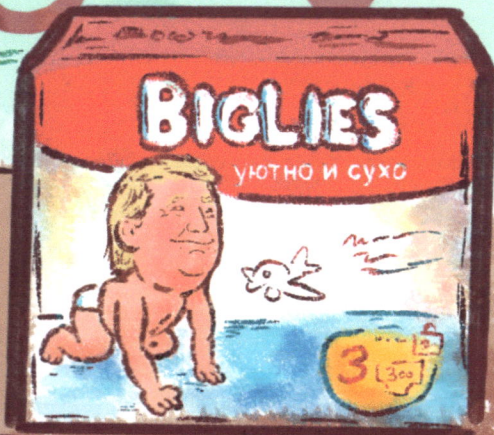

Count some sheep...
off you go...
at long @!#?&$@! last...
to sleep.

At last, some peace and quiet.
Just me, a good book and **DING DONG**
Oh geez. Come on. This freaking guy.
Oh well, take me away. No more meltdowns. No more tweets.
Maybe I, too, can finally get some sleep.

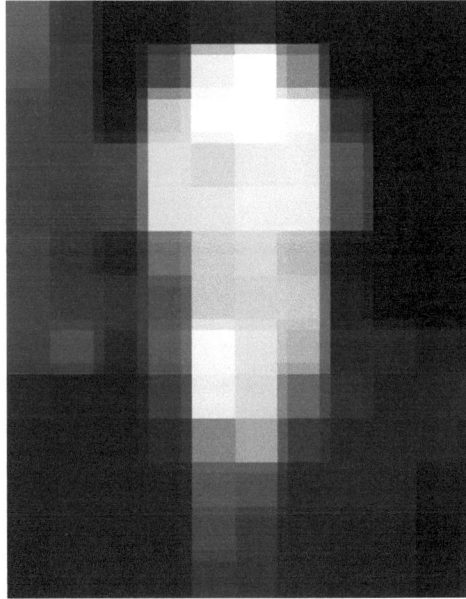

About the Author

John Spreincer McKellyanne Huckamucci is ███████████████ ████████████████████████████████████ ██████ hopes to have a career in cable news one day. ███████ lives in ███████████████., and this is ████ first book.

www.ingramcontent.com/pod-product-compliance
Lightning Source LLC
Chambersburg PA
CBHW041553030426

42336CB00004B/57